HISTORY OF INVENTIONS

Communication Technology

From Smoke Signals to Smartphones

Tracey Kelly

BROWN BEAR BOOKS

Published by Brown Bear Books Ltd
4877 N. Circulo Bujia
Tucson, AZ 85718
USA

and

Unit 1/D, Leroy House
436 Essex Rd
London N1 3QP
UK

ISBN 978-1-78121-457-2 (library bound)
ISBN 978-1-78121-473-2 (paperback)

Library of Congress Cataloging-in-Publication Data available on request

Text: Tracey Kelly
Designer: Supriya Sahai
Design Manager: Keith Davis
Picture Manager: Sophie Mortimer
Editorial Director: Lindsey Lowe
Children's Publisher: Anne O'Daly

Picture Credits
Front Cover: iStock: Polke.
123rf: bloomua, 19; Getty Images: Hemera Technologies/RF, 9; iStock: Adrio, 7, Jaka Azman, 14, Kenneth Cheung, 17, Kalinin Iakov, 10, maumapho, 16, real444, 18; Metropolitan Museum of Art: 4; Public Domain: Corbis, 15, Press Release, 20, State Library of Queensland, 8, Wireless Press, New York, 11; Shutterstock: Andrey Kuzmin 5l, Lawrence Roberg, 13, Kirill Smimov, 12, Peter Sobolev, 21; US Government: United States Navy photograph, 5tr.
Key: t=top, b=bottom, c=center, l=left, r=right

Brown Bear Books has made every attempt to contact the copyright holder.
If you have any information, please contact: licensing@brownbearbooks.co.uk

Manufactured in the United States of America
CPSIA compliance information: Batch#AG/5624

Websites
The website addresses in this book were valid at the time of going to press. However, it is possible that contents or addresses may change following publication of this book. No responsibility for any such changes can be accepted by the author or the publisher. Readers should be supervised when they access the Internet.

Contents

Keeping in Touch

People have always "talked" to each other from far away. But they did not always have telephones. They used different ways to get in touch with each other.

Smoke Signals
Native Americans used smoke signals. They built a fire on a hill. They waved a wet blanket over the fire in patterns. The smoke rose in the air. People far away could "read" the patterns it made.

Semaphore

Sailors used colored flags to signal to other ships. The flags were waved in patterns. The patterns made up words. This is called semaphore.

Sealed Letters

People sent sealed letters. They dripped hot wax on the envelope. They pressed their ring into the wax. This "sealed" the letter.

Read on ... to learn about how people have kept in touch through the years.

Telegraph

The telegraph sent messages over long distances. It used electric signals. The signals went through a wire. These messages used a special code. It was called Morse code.

Morse Code

You tapped in dots and dashes using a key. Each letter or number had a different pattern. Can you tap your name?

A	• —	K	— • —	U	• • —	1	• — — — —
B	— • • •	L	• — • •	V	• • • —	2	• • — — —
C	— • — •	M	— —	W	• — —	3	• • • — —
D	— • •	N	— •	X	— • • —	4	• • • • —
E	•	O	— — —	Y	— • — —	5	• • • • •
F	• • — •	P	• — — •	Z	— — • •	6	— • • • •
G	— — •	Q	— — • —			7	— — • • •
H	• • • •	R	• — •			8	— — — • •
I	• •	S	• • •			9	— — — — •
J	• — — —	T	—			0	— — — — —

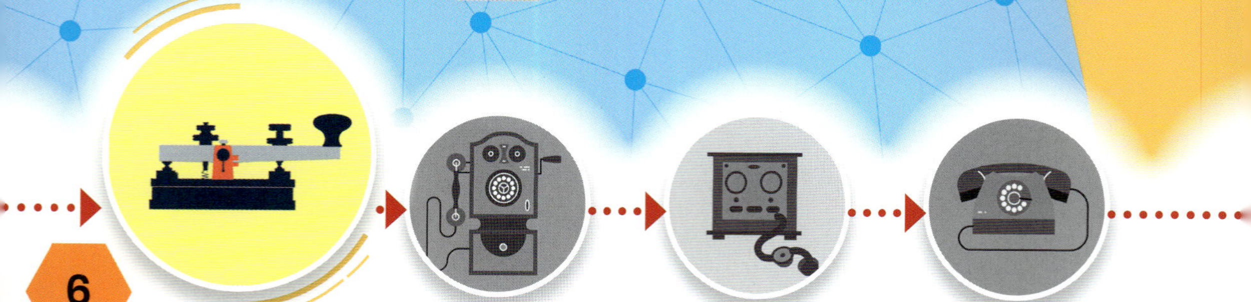

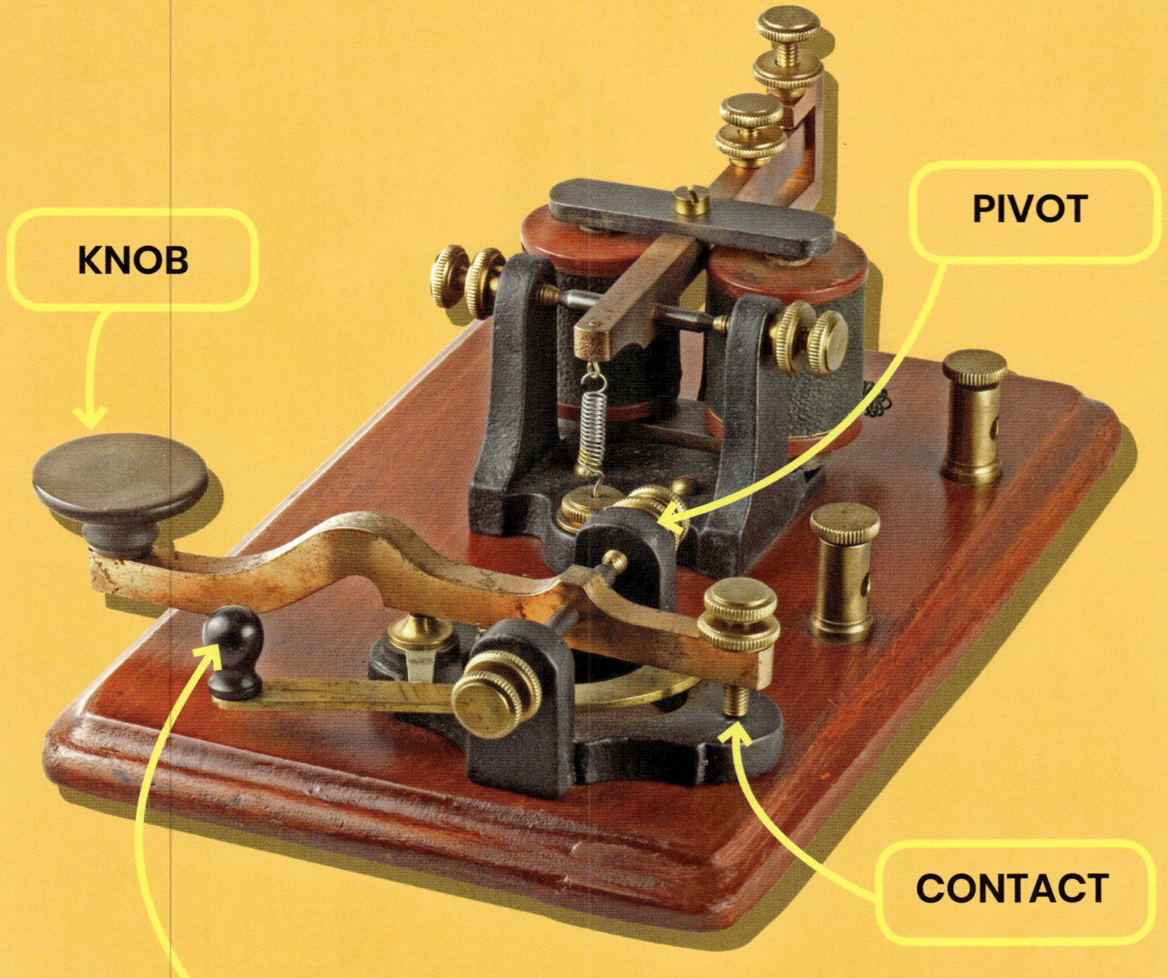

Morse code spelled out words. People read your message at another telegraph. They sent a message back.

Box Phone

Early phones were big and heavy. They hung from the wall. You could not call someone yourself. You had to speak to an operator.

Telephone Exchange
Telephone lines went to a telephone exchange. You said who you wanted to talk to. The operator connected your phone to theirs.

Old Telephone
You spoke into the mouthpiece. You listened through the earpiece. Bells rang when a call came through.

Radio Waves

Radiotelephones used radio wave signals. Messages were sent as pulses. You could call someone far away. They could hear your voice.

1915 Radio Call
A voice message was sent from a radio station in Arlington, Virginia. It reached the Eiffel Tower in Paris, France! It had traveled 3,800 miles (6,115 kilometers).

The machine had a transmitter that sent radio waves. You spoke into the mouthpiece. You listened through headphones.

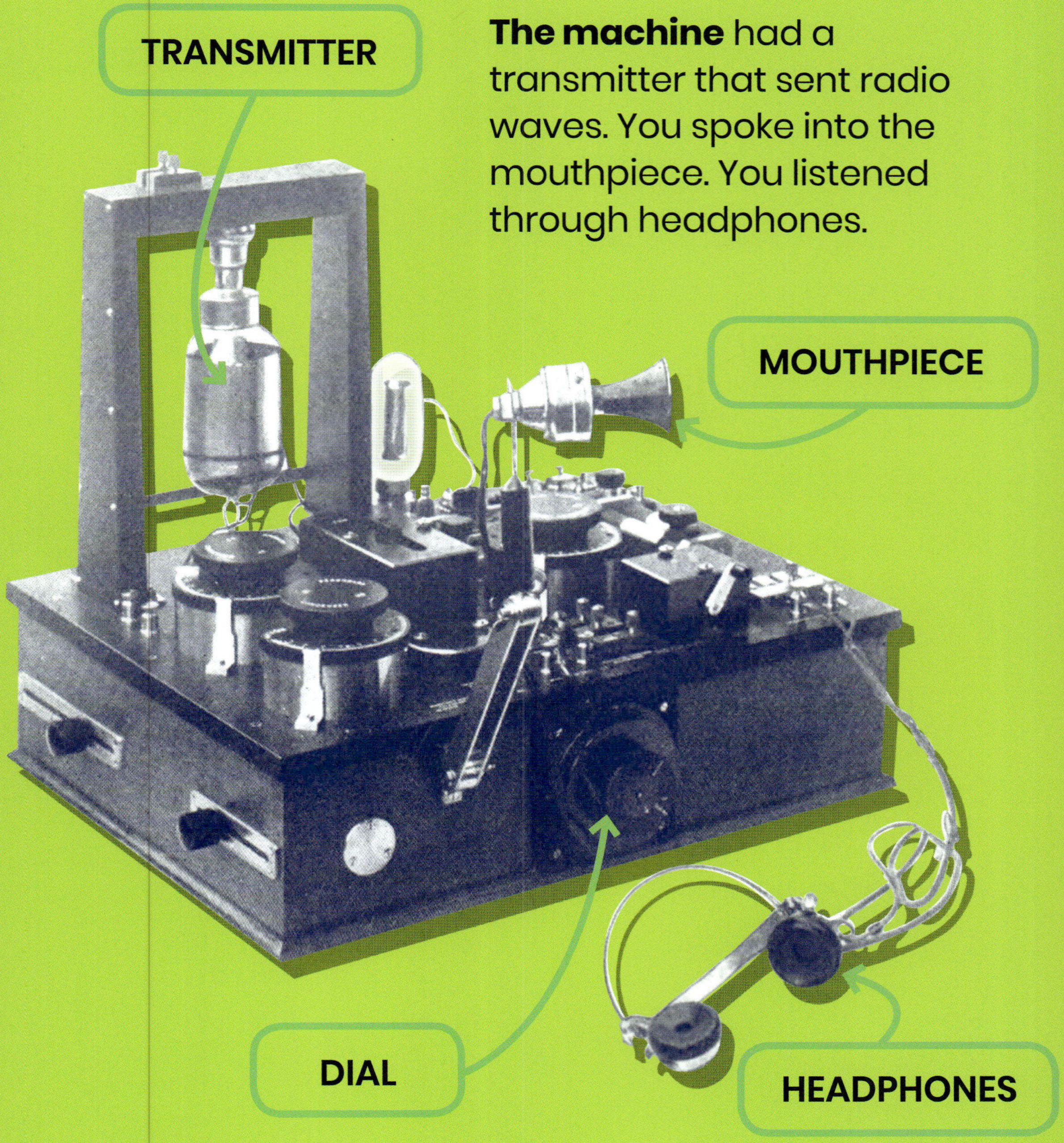

Dial Up

People began using phones with number dials. Each house was given a phone number. You didn't need an operator to make a call.

Dial Phone
Dial phones had ten numbers. You put your finger in a circle, then spun it around. You dialed a phone number.

Touch-Tone Phones

Later, touch-tone phones were used. You pushed buttons to make a call. Each button made a different sound.

Computers

Early computers used modems to reach other computers. Modems use sound signals to send messages. The signals go along telephone lines. They connect to other computers.

Wi-Fi

Wi-Fi connects computers to the Internet. But it doesn't need a wire to connect. It uses radio waves.

Electronic Mail

Emails are electronic messages. You type an email on your computer. Then, you press send. Your friend can send an email back.

Cell Phone

The first cell phones were big and heavy. They had an antenna. You pushed numbers on the keypad. Today's cell phones are much smaller and lighter.

Cell Network

Cell phones are connected to a network. The network has cell towers that send signals. They connect phones using radio waves.

The microphone was at the bottom. You talked into it. Your ear pressed up to the top. You heard your friend's voice through the speaker.

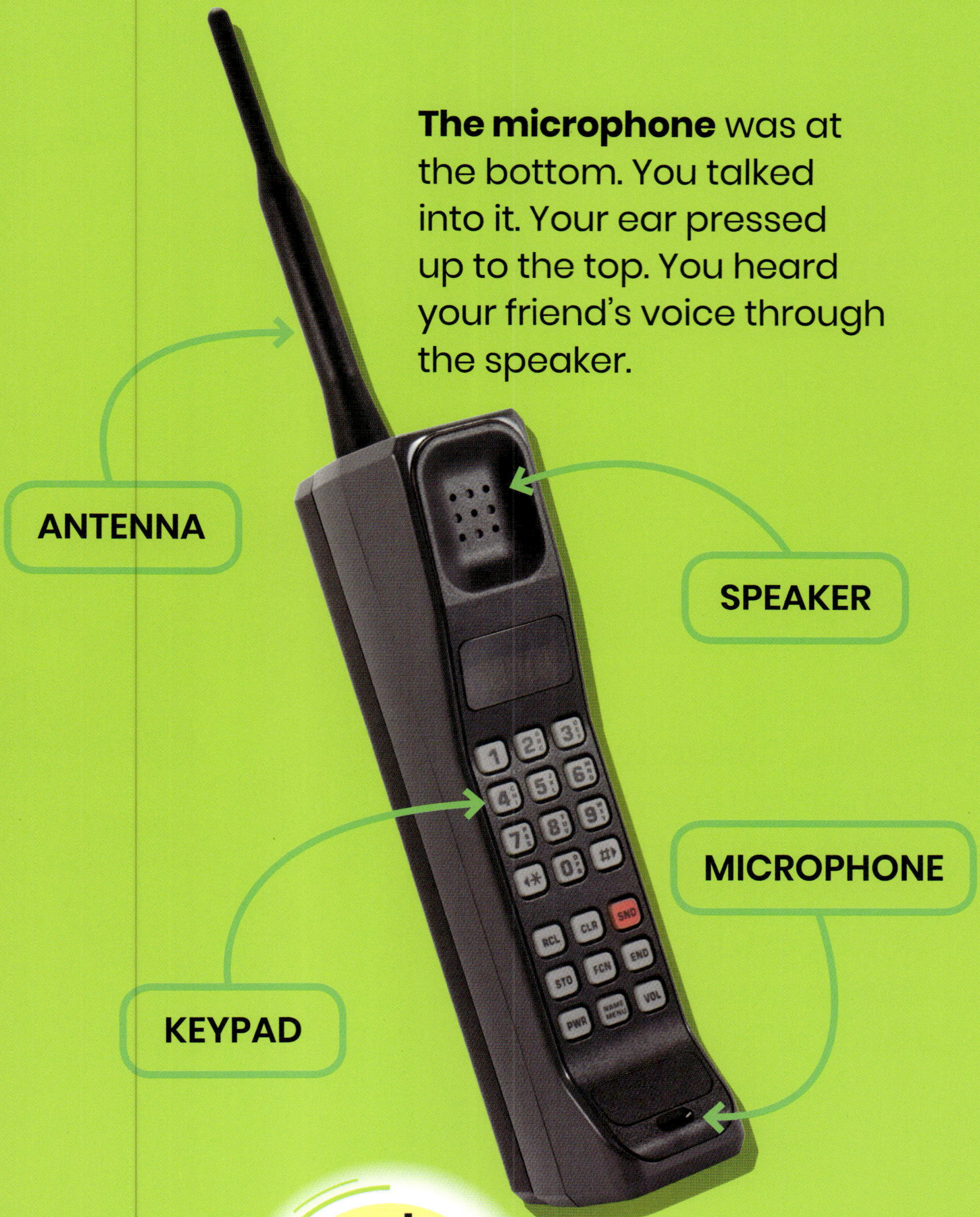

Smartphone

Modern phones are called smartphones. They do a lot more than make calls! Smartphones are like tiny computers. You can send emails or search the Internet.

Mini Computers
Smartphones have a camera to take photos. You can download apps to play games. You can read a book or listen to music. You can watch a movie!

Buttons turn the phone on and off. The home button takes you back to the start screen.

Future Phones

New smartphones are being invented. They will have even more apps. Some will translate languages. What do you think phones will do next?

Bracelet Phone
A bracelet phone is being tested. It will send the picture of a screen to your arm. So, you can use apps by pressing your skin. You can type in emails, too.

Flexible Phone
Scientists are making bendable phones. These phones won't break if you drop them.

Timeline

from 200 BCE	Native Americans and other early peoples use smoke signals.
1790s CE	Semaphore is used to send messages.
pre-1800s	Sealed letters are sent between people.
1837	The telegraph system is invented.
1876	The first telephone is used.
early 1900s	The radiotelephone sends voice messages. It uses radio waves.
1920s	The dial phone is used.
1963	The first touch-tone phones are used.
1960s	Computers are used in businesses.
1970s	The first "@" emails are sent.
1980s	The first cell phones are used.
1990s	Cell phones are small enough for everyone to use.
1997	Wi-Fi is first used in homes.
2007	Smartphones are first used.
2010s	Wristwatch phones become popular.

Glossary

app A small program on a smartphone or tablet.

cell phone A telephone that uses a radio system to connect to other phones.

computer An electronic device for storing and using data.

data Information that is stored on a computer.

Internet A global network that connects computers.

modem A device that connects computers using a telephone line.

Morse code A code using dots and dashes that stand for letters and numbers.

radio waves Electronic waves used for sending messages long distance.

smartphone A cell phone with apps, a camera, and a voice recorder.

telegraph A system for sending messages by electronic wire.

telephone exchange A device where many telephone lines connect.

touch-tone phone A phone that uses buttons to tap in numbers.

Wi-Fi A wireless connection to the Internet.

Further Resources

Books

Alexander Graham Bell Barbara Kramer, National Geographic Children's Books, 2015

Story of Coding James Floyd Kelly, Dorling Kindersley, 2017

Thomas Edison Barbara Kramer, National Geographic Children's Books, 2014

Websites

Find out all about Alexander Graham Bell, who invented the telephone: www.ducksters.com/biography/alexander_graham_bell.php

Read all about the history of telephones: kids.kiddle.co/Telephone

Index